SIMPLICITY

PERSONAL INFORMATION

NAME

SURNAME

ADDRESS

HOME TELEPHONE   MOBILE

E-MAIL

BUSINESS ADDRESS

BUSINESS TELEPHONE   FAX

E-MAIL

WEBSITE

IN CASE OF EMERGENCY, PLEASE CONTACT

PAULO COELHO

SIMPLICITY

2022

Vintage International
Vintage Books
A Division of Penguin Random House LLC
New York

SIMPLICIDAD

How to begin?
Silence. The hubbub of life outside
seems to pause in the night.
Words, ideas, memories, and stories
are the paths that guide my steps.

2022

JANUARY

	S	M	T	W	T	F	S
52							1
1	2	3	4	5	6	7	8
2	9	10	11	12	13	14	15
3	16	17	18	19	20	21	22
4	23	24	25	26	27	28	29
5	30	31					

FEBRUARY

	S	M	T	W	T	F	S
5			1	2	3	4	5
6	6	7	8	9	10	11	12
7	13	14	15	16	17	18	19
8	20	21	22	23	24	25	26
9	27	28					

MARCH

	S	M	T	W	T	F	S
9			1	2	3	4	5
10	6	7	8	9	10	11	12
11	13	14	15	16	17	18	19
12	20	21	22	23	24	25	26
13	27	28	29	30	31		

APRIL

	S	M	T	W	T	F	S
13						1	2
14	3	4	5	6	7	8	9
15	10	11	12	13	14	15	16
16	17	18	19	20	21	22	23
17	24	25	26	27	28	29	30

MAY

	S	M	T	W	T	F	S
18	1	2	3	4	5	6	7
19	8	9	10	11	12	13	14
20	15	16	17	18	19	20	21
21	22	23	24	25	26	27	28
22	29	30	31				

JUNE

	S	M	T	W	T	F	S
22				1	2	3	4
23	5	6	7	8	9	10	11
24	12	13	14	15	16	17	18
25	19	20	21	22	23	24	25
26	26	27	28	29	30		

JULY

	S	M	T	W	T	F	S
26						1	2
27	3	4	5	6	7	8	9
28	10	11	12	13	14	15	16
29	17	18	19	20	21	22	23
30	24	25	26	27	28	29	30
31	31						

AUGUST

	S	M	T	W	T	F	S
31		1	2	3	4	5	6
32	7	8	9	10	11	12	13
33	14	15	16	17	18	19	20
34	21	22	23	24	25	26	27
35	28	29	30	31			

SEPTEMBER

	S	M	T	W	T	F	S
35					1	2	3
36	4	5	6	7	8	9	10
37	11	12	13	14	15	16	17
38	18	19	20	21	22	23	24
39	25	26	27	28	29	30	

OCTOBER

	S	M	T	W	T	F	S
39							1
40	2	3	4	5	6	7	8
41	9	10	11	12	13	14	15
42	16	17	18	19	20	21	22
43	23	24	25	26	27	28	29
44	30	31					

NOVEMBER

	S	M	T	W	T	F	S
44			1	2	3	4	5
45	6	7	8	9	10	11	12
46	13	14	15	16	17	18	19
47	20	21	22	23	24	25	26
48	27	28	29	30			

DECEMBER

	S	M	T	W	T	F	S
48					1	2	3
49	4	5	6	7	8	9	10
50	11	12	13	14	15	16	17
51	18	19	20	21	22	23	24
52	25	26	27	28	29	30	31

2023

JANUARY

S	M	T	W	T	F	S
1	**1**	2	3	3	5	6	7
2	**8**	9	10	11	12	13	14
3	**15**	**16**	17	18	19	20	21
4	**22**	23	24	25	26	27	28
5	**29**	30	31				

FEBRUARY

S	M	T	W	T	F	S
5				1	2	3	4
6	**5**	6	7	8	9	10	11
7	**12**	13	**14**	15	16	17	18
8	**19**	**20**	21	22	23	24	25
9	**26**	27	28				

MARCH

S	M	T	W	T	F	S
9				1	2	3	4
10	**5**	6	7	8	9	10	11
11	**12**	13	14	15	16	17	18
12	**19**	20	21	22	23	24	25
13	**26**	27	28	29	30	31	

APRIL

S	M	T	W	T	F	S
13							1
14	**2**	3	4	5	6	**7**	8
15	**9**	**10**	11	12	13	14	15
16	**16**	17	18	19	20	21	22
17	**23**	24	25	26	27	28	29
18	**30**						

MAY

S	M	T	W	T	F	S
18		1	2	3	4	5	6
19	**7**	8	9	10	11	12	13
20	**14**	15	16	17	18	19	20
21	**21**	22	23	24	25	26	27
22	**28**	**29**	30	31			

JUNE

S	M	T	W	T	F	S
22					1	2	3
23	**4**	5	6	7	8	9	10
24	**11**	12	13	14	15	16	17
25	**18**	19	20	21	22	23	24
26	**25**	26	27	28	29	30	

JULY

S	M	T	W	T	F	S
26							1
27	**2**	3	**4**	5	6	7	8
28	**9**	10	11	12	13	14	15
29	**16**	17	18	19	20	21	22
30	**23**	24	25	26	27	28	29
31	**30**	31					

AUGUST

S	M	T	W	T	F	S
31		1	2	3	4	5	
32	**6**	7	8	9	10	11	12
33	**13**	14	15	16	17	18	19
34	**20**	21	22	23	24	25	26
35	**27**	28	29	30	31		

SEPTEMBER

S	M	T	W	T	F	S
35						1	2
36	**3**	**4**	5	6	7	8	9
37	**10**	11	12	13	14	15	16
38	**17**	18	19	20	21	22	23
39	**24**	25	26	27	28	29	30

OCTOBER

S	M	T	W	T	F	S
40	**1**	2	3	3	5	6	7
41	**8**	**9**	10	11	12	13	14
42	**15**	16	17	18	19	20	21
43	**22**	23	24	25	26	27	28
44	**29**	30	31				

NOVEMBER

S	M	T	W	T	F	S
44				1	2	3	4
45	**5**	6	7	8	9	10	**11**
46	**12**	13	14	15	16	17	18
47	**19**	20	21	22	**23**	24	25
48	**26**	27	28	29	30		

DECEMBER

S	M	T	W	T	F	S
48						1	2
49	**3**	4	5	6	7	8	9
50	**10**	11	12	13	14	15	16
51	**17**	18	19	20	21	22	23
52	**24**	**25**	26	27	28	29	30
1	**31**						

JANUARY 2022

	S	M	T	W	T	F	S
52							**1**
1	**2**	3	4	5	6	7	8
2	**9**	10	11	12	13	14	15
3	**16**	**17**	18	19	20	21	22
4	**23**	24	25	26	27	28	29
5	**30**	31					

1   New Year's Day
17   Martin Luther King Jr. Day

FEBRUARY 2022

	S	M	T	W	T	F	S
5			1	2	3	4	5
6	**6**	7	8	9	10	11	12
7	**13**	**14**	15	16	17	18	19
8	**20**	**21**	22	23	24	25	26
9	**27**	28					

14   Valentine's Day
21   Presidents' Day

MARCH 2022

	S	M	T	W	T	F	S
9			1	2●	3	4	5
10	**6**	7	8	9	10◗	11	12
11	**13**	14	15	16	17	18○	19
12	**20**	21	22	23	24	25◑	26
13	**27**	28	29	30	31		

APRIL 2022

	S	M	T	W	T	F	S
13						1●	2
14	**3**	4	5	6	7	8	9◗
15	**10**	11	12	13	14	**15**	16○
16	**17**	**18**	19	20	21	22	23◑
17	**24**	25	26	27	28	29	30●

15 Good Friday
17 Easter Sunday
18 Easter Monday

MAY 2022

	S	M	T	W	T	F	S
18	**1**	2	3	4	5	6	7
19	**8**◗	9	10	11	12	13	14
20	**15**○	16	17	18	19	20	21
21	**22**◑	23	24	25	26	27	28
22	**29**	**30**●	31				

8 **Mother's Day**
30 **Memorial Day**

JUNE 2022

	S	M	T	W	T	F	S
22				1	2	3	4
23	**5**	6	**7**◗	8	9	10	11
24	**12**	13	**14**○	15	16	17	18
25	**19**	20◑	21	22	23	24	25
26	**26**	27	28●	29	30		

19 **Father's day**

JULY 2022

	S	M	T	W	T	F	S
26						1	2
27	**3**	**4**	5	6◐	7	8	9
28	**10**	11	12	13○ 14		15	16
29	**17**	18	19	20◑ 21		22	23
30	**24**	25	26	27	28● 29		30
31	**31**						

4   **Independence Day**

AUGUST 2022

	S	M	T	W	T	F	S
31		1	2	3	4	5◐	6
32	**7**	8	9	10	11	12○ 13	
33	**14**	15	16	17	18◑ 19		20
34	**21**	22	23	24	25	26	27●
35	**28**	29	30	31			

PLANNING ANNUAL 2022

SEPTEMBER 2022

	S	M	T	W	T	F	S
35					1	2	3◗
36	**4**	**5**	6	7	8	9	10○
37	**11**	12	13	14	15	16	17◗
38	**18**	19	20	21	22	23	24
39	**25**●	26	27	28	29	30	

5   **Labor Day**

OCTOBER 2022

	S	M	T	W	T	F	S
39							1
40	**2**◗	3	4	5	6	7	8
41	**9**○	**10**	11	12	13	14	15
42	**16**	17◗	18	19	20	21	22
43	**23**	24●	25	26	27	28	29
44	**30**	31					

10   **Columbus Day**

NOVEMBER 2022

	S	M	T	W	T	F	S
44			1	2	3	4	5
45	6	7	8	9	10	11	12
46	13	14	15	16	17	18	19
47	20	21	22	23 24	25	26
48	27	28	29	30			

11   Veterans Day
24   Thanksgiving Day

DECEMBER 2022

	S	M	T	W	T	F	S
48					1	2	3
49	4	5	6	7	8	9	10
50	11	12	13	14	15	16	17
51	18	19	20	21	22	23	24
52	25	26	27	28	29	30	31

25   Christmas Day

JANUARY

Creation

Teaching merely shows us what is possible. Learning is making things possible for yourself.

THE PILGRIMAGE

---

1 | Saturday

The miracle of Creation came about by itself.

MAKTUB

52							1
1	**2**	3	4	5	6	7	8
2	**9**	10	11	12	13	14	15
3	**16**	**17**	18	19	20	21	22
4	**23**	24	25	26	27	28	29
5	**30**	31					

2 | Sunday

3 | Monday

4 | Tuesday

It isn't explanations that carry us forward,
it's our desire to go on.

BRIDA

52							**1**
1	**2**	3	4	5	6	7	8
2	**9**	10	11	12	13	14	15
3	**16**	**17**	18	19	20	21	22
4	**23**	24	25	26	27	28	29
5	**30**	31					

5 | Wednesday

6 | Thursday

7 Friday

8 Saturday

A life without cause is a life without effect.

ALEPH

52							1
1	**2**	3	4	5	6	7	8
2	**9**	10	11	12	13	14	15
3	**16**	**17**	18	19	20	21	22
4	**23**	24	25	26	27	28	29
5	**30**	31					

9 | Sunday

10 Monday

11 Tuesday

Defeat ends when we launch into another battle.
Failure has no end; it is a lifetime choice.

MANUSCRIPT FOUND IN ACCRA

52							**1**
1	**2**	3	4	5	6	7	8
2	**9**	10	11	12	13	14	15
3	**16**	**17**	18	19	20	21	22
4	**23**	24	25	26	27	28	29
5	**30**	31					

12 | Wednesday

13 | Thursday

14 Friday

15 Saturday

Only those who find life are capable
of finding treasures.

THE ALCHEMIST

Week 3

52							**1**
1	**2**	3	4	5	6	7	8
2	**9**	10	11	12	13	14	15
3	**16**	**17**	18	19	20	21	22
4	**23**	24	25	26	27	28	29
5	**30**	31					

16 | Sunday

17 Monday

18 Tuesday

God's work is to be found in the smallest
details of Creation.

CHRONICLE – THE CIRCLE OF JOY

Week 3

52							1
1	**2**	3	4	5	6	7	8
2	**9**	10	11	12	13	14	15
3	**16**	**17**	18	19	20	21	22
4	**23**	24	25	26	27	28	29
5	**30**	31					

19 Wednesday

20 Thursday

21 Friday

22 Saturday

Love is enough to justify a whole existence.

THE WITCH OF PORTOBELLO

52							**1**
1	**2**	3	4	5	6	7	8
2	**9**	10	11	12	13	14	15
3	**16**	**17**	18	19	20	21	22
4	**23**	24	25	26	27	28	29
5	**30**	31					

23 | Sunday

24 Monday

25 Tuesday

The essence of Creation is one and one alone.
And that essence is called Love.

BRIDA

JANUARY

52							**1**
1	**2**	3	4	5	6	7	8
2	**9**	10	11	12	13	14	15
3	**16**	**17**	18	19	20	21	22
4	**23**	24	25	26	27	28	29
5	**30**	31					

26 | Wednesday

27 | Thursday

28 Friday

29 Saturday

So what we call "life" is a train with many carriages.
Sometimes we're in one, sometimes we're in another, and sometimes
we cross between them, when we dream or allow ourselves to be
swept away by the extraordinary.

ALEPH

JANUARY

52							1
1	**2**	3	4	5	6	7	8
2	**9**	10	11	12	13	14	15
3	**16**	**17**	18	19	20	21	22
4	**23**	24	25	26	27	28	29
5	**30**	31					

30 | Sunday

31 | Monday

Small things are responsible for great changes.

MANUSCRIPT FOUND IN ACCRA

52							**1**
1	**2**	3	4	5	6	7	8
2	**9**	10	11	12	13	14	15
3	**16**	**17**	18	19	20	21	22
4	**23**	24	25	26	27	28	29
5	**30**	31					

FEBRUARY

Humility

What is a teacher? I would
say that it is not someone who
teaches something, but someone who
inspires students to do their best to
discover a knowledge that is already
there in their soul.

THE ARCHER

1 | Tuesday

Every person on Earth has a gift. In some,
the gift manifests itself spontaneously; others
have to work hard to find it.

BY THE RIVER PIEDRA I SAT DOWN AND WEPT

		1	2	3	4	5
5						
6	**6**	7	8	9	10	11	12
7	**13**	**14**	15	16	17	18	19
8	**20**	**21**	22	23	24	25	26
9	**27**	28				

2 Wednesday

3 Thursday

4 | Friday

5 | Saturday

But only the person who accepts God's plan
with humility and courage knows that he is
on the right road.

MANUSCRIPT FOUND IN ACCRA

5			1	2	3	4	5
6	**6**	7	8	9	10	11	12
7	**13**	**14**	15	16	17	18	19
8	**20**	**21**	22	23	24	25	26
9	**27**	28					

6 | Sunday

7 Monday

8 Tuesday

Whenever you want to find out
about something, plunge straight in.

BRIDA

FEBRUARY

			1	2	3	4	5
5			1	2	3	4	5
6	**6**	7	8	9	10	11	12
7	**13**	**14**	15	16	17	18	19
8	**20**	**21**	22	23	24	25	26
9	**27**	28					

9 Wednesday

10 Thursday

11 | Friday

12 | Saturday

Let us be absolutely clear about one thing:
we must not confuse humility with false
modesty or servility.

CHRONICLE – STORIES ABOUT TRUE HUMILITY

		1	2	3	4	5
5						
6	**6**	7	8	9	10	11	12
7	**13**	**14**	15	16	17	18	19
8	**20**	**21**	22	23	24	25	26
9	**27**	28					

13 Sunday

14 Monday

15 Tuesday

Life was made up of simple things; he was weary
of all the years he had spent searching for
something, though quite what he didn't know.

ELEVEN MINUTES

FEBRUARY

		1	2	3	4	5
5						
6	**6**	7	8	9	10	11	12
7	**13**	**14**	15	16	17	18	19
8	**20**	**21**	22	23	24	25	26
9	**27**	28					

16 | Wednesday

17 | Thursday

18 Friday

19 Saturday

In order to forget the rules, you must know
them and respect them.

THE WITCH OF PORTOBELLO

Week 8

		1	2	3	4	5
5						
6	**6**	7	8	9	10	11	12
7	**13**	**14**	15	16	17	18	19
8	**20**	**21**	22	23	24	25	26
9	**27**	28				

20 | Sunday

21 | Monday

22 | Tuesday

Willpower alone cannot transform you. Love can.

THE SUPREME GIFT

Week 8

5		1	2	3	4	5
6	**6**	7	8	9	10	11	12
7	**13**	**14**	15	16	17	18	19
8	**20**	**21**	22	23	24	25	26
9	**27**	28				

23 | Wednesday

24 | Thursday

25 Friday

26 Saturday

Success does not come from having one's work
recognized by others. It is the fruit of a seed
that you lovingly planted.

MANUSCRIPT FOUND IN ACCRA

Week 9

		1	2	3	4	5
5						
6	**6**	7	8	9	10	11	12
7	**13**	**14**	15	16	17	18	19
8	**20**	**21**	22	23	24	25	26
9	**27**	28					

27 | Sunday

28 Monday

Discipline is important, but it needs to leave
doors and windows open to intuition
and the unexpected.

MANUSCRIPT FOUND IN ACCRA

Week 9

5			1	2	3	4	5
6	**6**	7	8	9	10	11	12
7	**13**	**14**	15	16	17	18	19
8	**20**	**21**	22	23	24	25	26
9	**27**	28					

MARCH

Silence

Music isn't a succession of notes. It's the constant movement of a note between sound and silence.

ALEPH

1 Tuesday

Live everything as intensely as you can and keep
whatever you felt as a gift from God.

BRIDA

Week 9

9		1	2	3	4	5
10	**6**	7	8	9	10	11	12
11	**13**	14	15	16	17	18	19
12	**20**	21	22	23	24	25	26
13	**27**	28	29	30	31		

2 Wednesday

3 Thursday

4 | Friday

5 | Saturday

The desert is so vast, and the horizons so distant,
that they make us feel very small and lost
for words.

THE ALCHEMIST

Week 10

MARCH

9		1	2	3	4	5
10	**6**	7	8	9	10	11	12
11	**13**	14	15	16	17	18	19
12	**20**	21	22	23	24	25	26
13	**27**	28	29	30	31		

6 | Sunday

7 | Monday

8 | Tuesday

Love is an act of faith in another person,
and its face should always be veiled in mystery.

THE SPY

		1	2	3	4	5
9						
10	**6**	7	8	9	10	11	12
11	**13**	14	15	16	17	18	19
12	**20**	21	22	23	24	25	26
13	**27**	28	29	30	31	

9 Wednesday

10 Thursday

11 | Friday

12 | Saturday

Respect the time between sowing and harvesting.

MANUSCRIPT FOUND IN ACCRA

Week 11

9		1	2	3	4	5
10	**6**	7	8	9	10	11	12
11	**13**	14	15	16	17	18	19
12	**20**	21	22	23	24	25	26
13	**27**	28	29	30	31		

13 | Sunday

14 Monday

15 Tuesday

Only the person who listens to the sounds of the
present moment can make the right decisions.

THE PILGRIMAGE

MARCH

9		1	2	3	4	5
10	**6**	7	8	9	10	11	12
11	**13**	14	15	16	17	18	19
12	**20**	21	22	23	24	25	26
13	**27**	28	29	30	31		

16 | Wednesday

17 | Thursday

18 Friday

19 Saturday

Silence may be translated into words.

HIPPIE

MARCH

			1	2	3	4	5
9							
10	**6**	7	8	9	10	11	12
11	**13**	14	15	16	17	18	19
12	**20**	21	22	23	24	25	26
13	**27**	28	29	30	31		

20 | Sunday

21 | Monday

22 | Tuesday

Only cowards hide behind silence.

THE DEVIL AND MISS PRYM

M A R C H

		1	2	3	4	5
9						
10	**6**	7	8	9	10	11	12
11	**13**	14	15	16	17	18	19
12	**20**	21	22	23	24	25	26
13	**27**	28	29	30	31		

23 | Wednesday

24 | Thursday

25 Friday

26 Saturday

Sometimes, in the silence of our hearts, we say to
ourselves: "How good it would be to be free,
to have no commitments."

THE ZAHIR

27 | Sunday

28 Monday

29 Tuesday

He listened to his heart. And the desert listened to
his fear. They both spoke the same language.

THE ALCHEMIST

MARCH

9		1	2	3	4	5
10	**6** 7	8	9	10	11	12
11	**13** 14	15	16	17	18	19
12	**20** 21	22	23	24	25	26
13	**27** 28	29	30	31		

30 | Wednesday

31 | Thursday

APRIL

Greatness

This is the most difficult
moment in anyone's life—when
we can see what the good fight is,
but feel incapable of changing
our life and going into battle.

THE PILGRIMAGE

1 | Friday

2 | Saturday

And what makes you think that we, with our path
and our dedication, understand the Universe
any better than other people?

BRIDA

13						1	2
14	**3**	4	5	6	7	8	9
15	**10**	11	12	13	14	**15**	16
16	**17**	**18**	19	20	21	22	23
17	**24**	25	26	27	28	29	30

3 | Sunday

4 Monday

5 Tuesday

No heart has ever suffered when it goes in search of its
dreams, because every second of the search is a
second's encounter with God and with eternity.

THE ALCHEMIST

13						1	2
14	**3**	4	5	6	7	8	9
15	**10**	11	12	13	14	**15**	16
16	**17**	**18**	19	20	21	22	23
17	**24**	25	26	27	28	29	30

6 Wednesday

7 Thursday

8 Friday

9 Saturday

The art of peace is unbeatable, because no one is
fighting against anyone, only themselves. If you
conquer yourself, then you will conquer the world.

ALEPH

APRIL

						1	2
13						1	2
14	**3**	4	5	6	7	**8**	9
15	**10**	11	12	13	14	**15**	16
16	**17**	**18**	19	20	21	22	23
17	**24**	25	26	27	28	29	30

10 | Sunday

11 Monday

12 Tuesday

When we love and believe in something from the bottom
of our heart, we feel ourselves to be stronger than the world,
and are filled with a serenity that is based on the certainty
that nothing can shake our faith.

THE PILGRIMAGE

APRIL

						1	2
13							
14	**3**	4	5	6	7	8	9
15	**10**	11	12	13	14	**15**	16
16	**17**	**18**	19	20	21	22	23
17	**24**	25	26	27	28	29	30

13 | Wednesday

14 | Thursday

15 Friday

16 Saturday

Wanting to be the same as everyone else is a
grave error, because it's a distortion of nature.

VERONIKA DECIDES TO DIE

						1	2
13						1	2
14	**3**	4	5	6	7	8	9
15	**10**	11	12	13	14	**15**	16
16	**17**	**18**	19	20	21	22	23
17	**24**	25	26	27	28	29	30

17 Sunday

18 Monday

19 Tuesday

Anyone who does not share his moments of joy
and discouragement with others will never fully
know his own qualities and his own defects.

MANUSCRIPT FOUND IN ACCRA

APRIL

13						1	2
14	**3**	4	5	6	7	8	9
15	**10**	11	12	13	14	**15**	16
16	**17**	**18**	19	20	21	22	23
17	**24**	25	26	27	28	29	30

20 Wednesday

21 Thursday

22 | Friday

23 | Saturday

The most sophisticated things in the world are
precisely those within the reach of everyone.

ALEPH

APRIL

13						1	2
14	**3**	4	5	6	7	8	9
15	**10**	11	12	13	14	**15**	16
16	**17**	**18**	19	20	21	22	23
17	**24**	25	26	27	28	29	30

24 | Sunday

25 | Monday

_____

26 | Tuesday

_____

Our human condition makes us tend to share only
the best of ourselves, because we are always
searching for love and approval.

THE ZAHIR

APRIL

13						1	2
14	**3**	4	5	6	7	8	9
15	**10**	11	12	13	14	**15**	16
16	**17**	**18**	19	20	21	22	23
17	**24**	25	26	27	28	29	30

27 Wednesday

28 Thursday

29 | Friday

30 | Saturday

The simple things in life are the most
extraordinary.

THE ALCHEMIST

13						1	2
14	**3**	4	5	6	7	8	9
15	**10**	11	12	13	14	**15**	16
16	**17**	**18**	19	20	21	22	23
17	**24**	25	26	27	28	29	30

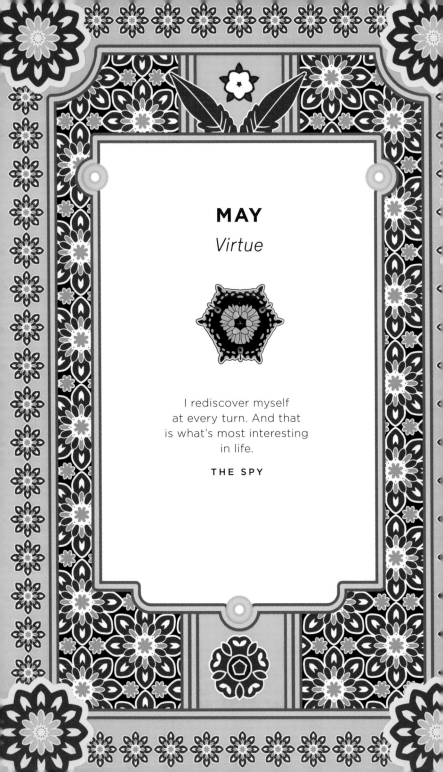

MAY

Virtue

I rediscover myself
at every turn. And that
is what's most interesting
in life.

THE SPY

The first great virtue of those seeking
the spiritual path: courage.

THE VALKYRIES

18	**1**	2	3	4	5	6	7
19	**8**	9	10	11	12	13	14
20	**15**	16	17	18	19	20	21
21	**22**	23	24	25	26	27	28
22	**29**	**30**	31				

1 | Sunday

2 Monday

3 Tuesday

I wish I didn't have to control my heart.

BY THE RIVER PIEDRA I SAT DOWN AND WEPT

Week 18

18	**1**	2	3	4	5	6	7
19	**8**	9	10	11	12	13	14
20	**15**	16	17	18	19	20	21
21	**22**	23	24	25	26	27	28
22	**29**	**30**	31				

4 | Wednesday

5 | Thursday

6 Friday

7 Saturday

A life is never useless. Each soul that came down
to Earth is here for a reason.

MANUSCRIPT FOUND IN ACCRA

MAY

19	**1**	2	3	4	5	6	7
19	**8**	9	10	11	12	13	14
20	**15**	16	17	18	19	20	21
21	**22**	23	24	25	26	27	28
22	**29**	**30**	31				

8 | Sunday

9 | Monday

10 | Tuesday

Someone once said that the earth produces
enough to satisfy need, but not enough
to satisfy greed.

THE VALKYRIES

18	**1**	2	3	4	5	6	7
19	**8**	9	10	11	12	13	14
20	**15**	16	17	18	19	20	21
21	**22**	23	24	25	26	27	28
22	**29**	**30**	31				

11 | Wednesday

12 | Thursday

13 Friday

14 Saturday

A beginner who knows what he or she needs is
more intelligent than an absent-minded sage.

WARRIOR OF LIGHT

18	**1**	2	3	4	5	6	7
19	**8**	9	10	11	12	13	14
20	**15**	16	17	18	19	20	21
21	**22**	23	24	25	26	27	28
22	**29**	**30**	31				

15 Sunday

16 Monday

17 Tuesday

No one who truly loves someone
would destroy them or themselves.

ALEPH

18	**1**	2	3	4	5	6	7
19	**8**	9	10	11	12	13	14
20	**15**	16	17	18	19	20	21
21	**22**	23	24	25	26	27	28
22	**29**	**30**	31				

18 | Wednesday

19 | Thursday

20 | Friday

21 | Saturday

Disobedience can also be a virtue
when we know how to use it.

MANUSCRIPT FOUND IN ACCRA

MAY

18	**1**	2	3	4	5	6	7
19	**8**	9	10	11	12	13	14
20	**15**	16	17	18	19	20	21
21	**22**	23	24	25	26	27	28
22	**29**	**30**	31				

22 | Sunday

23 Monday

24 Tuesday

The most important thing in all human relationships is
conversation, but people don't talk anymore.

THE ZAHIR

M A Y

18	**1**	2	3	4	5	6	7
19	**8**	9	10	11	12	13	14
20	**15**	16	17	18	19	20	21
21	**22**	23	24	25	26	27	28
22	**29**	**30**	31				

25 Wednesday

26 Thursday

27 Friday

28 Saturday

When we least expect it, life sets us a challenge
to test our courage and willingness to change.

THE DEVIL AND MISS PRYM

MAY

29 | Sunday

30 | Monday

31 | Tuesday

There were certain times when one had to accept
the mystery, and understand that we each
have our own gift.

THE VALKYRIES

Week 22

18	**1**	2	3	4	5	6	7
19	**8**	9	10	11	12	13	14
20	**15**	16	17	18	19	20	21
21	**22**	23	24	25	26	27	28
22	**29**	**30**	31				

JUNE

Invisible

Not everyone needs
to feel happy all the time.
Besides, no one can be happy
all the time. I need to learn
to deal with the reality
of life.

ADULTERY

In order to penetrate the invisible world
and develop your powers, you have to live
in the present, the *here and now*.

THE VALKYRIES

22				1	2	3	4
23	**5**	6	7	8	9	10	11
24	**12**	13	14	15	16	17	18
25	**19**	20	21	22	23	24	25
26	**26**	27	28	29	30		

1 | Wednesday

2 | Thursday

3 Friday

4 Saturday

Everything in this world is sacred, and a grain
of sand can be a bridge to the invisible.

BRIDA

22				1	2	3	4
23	**5**	6	7	8	9	10	11
24	**12**	13	14	15	16	17	18
25	**19**	20	21	22	23	24	25
26	**26**	27	28	29	30		

5 Sunday

6 Monday

7 Tuesday

There exists a language that is beyond words.

THE ALCHEMIST

22				1	2	3	4
23	**5**	6	7	8	9	10	11
24	**12**	13	14	15	16	17	18
25	**19**	20	21	22	23	24	25
26	**26**	27	28	29	30		

8 Wednesday

9 Thursday

10 Friday

11 Saturday

Help us to continue onward despite the fear
and to accept the inexplicable despite our need to
explain and know everything.

MANUSCRIPT FOUND IN ACCRA

JUNE

					1	2	3	4
22								
23	**5**	6	7	8	9	10	11
24	**12**	13	14	15	16	17	18
25	**19**	20	21	22	23	24	25
26	**26**	27	28	29	30		

12 | Sunday

13 Monday

14 Tuesday

We will only fully understand the miracle of life
when we allow the unexpected to happen.

BY THE RIVER PIEDRA I SAT DOWN AND WEPT

JUNE

22			1	2	3	4
23	**5**	6	7	8	9	10	11
24	**12**	13	14	15	16	17	18
25	**19**	20	21	22	23	24	25
26	**26**	27	28	29	30		

15 Wednesday

16 Thursday

17 Friday

18 Saturday

Every human being knew, subconsciously,
that there was a bridge to the invisible, a bridge that
one could cross without fear.

THE VALKYRIES

J U N E

22			1	2	3	4
23	**5**	6	7	8	9	10	11
24	**12**	13	14	15	16	17	18
25	**19**	20	21	22	23	24	25
26	**26**	27	28	29	30		

19 Sunday

20 Monday

21 Tuesday

Faith shows us that we are never alone.

MANUSCRIPT FOUND IN ACCRA

JUNE

22				1	2	3	4
23	**5**	6	7	8	9	10	11
24	**12**	13	14	15	16	17	18
25	**19**	20	21	22	23	24	25
26	**26**	27	28	29	30		

22 | Wednesday

23 | Thursday

24 Friday

25 Saturday

If all the words were joined together, they wouldn't
make sense, or, at the very least, would be extremely
hard to decipher. Spaces are crucial.

THE WITCH OF PORTOBELLO

J U N E

22				1	2	3	4
23	**5**	6	7	8	9	10	11
24	**12**	13	14	15	16	17	18
25	**19**	20	21	22	23	24	25
26	**26**	27	28	29	30		

26 Sunday

27 Monday

28 Tuesday

Desire is not what you see, but what you imagine.

ELEVEN MINUTES

22				1	2	3	4
23	**5**	6	7	8	9	10	11
24	**12**	13	14	15	16	17	18
25	**19**	20	21	22	23	24	25
26	**26**	27	28	29	30		

29 Wednesday

30 Thursday

JULY

Patience

No one can judge.
We all know the extent of
our own suffering or the
total absence of meaning
in our lives.

VERONIKA DECIDES TO DIE

1 Friday

2 Saturday

Wait patiently for the right moment to act.
Do not let the next opportunity slip by you.

MANUSCRIPT FOUND IN ACCRA

26						1	2
27	**3**	**4**	5	6	7	8	9
28	**10**	11	12	13	14	15	16
29	**17**	18	19	20	21	22	23
30	**24**	25	26	27	28	29	30
31	**31**						

3 | Sunday

4 Monday

5 Tuesday

We have to seek for love wherever it may be,
even if that means hours, days, weeks of
disappointment and sadness.

BY THE RIVER PIEDRA I SAT DOWN AND WEPT

26						1	2
27	**3**	**4**	5	6	7	8	9
28	**10**	11	12	13	14	15	16
29	**17**	18	19	20	21	22	23
30	**24**	25	26	27	28	29	30
31	**31**						

6 Wednesday

7 Thursday

8 Friday

9 Saturday

Faith and love are beyond dispute.

BY THE RIVER PIEDRA I SAT DOWN AND WEPT

JULY

						1	2
26							
27	**3**	**4**	5	6	7	8	9
28	**10**	11	12	13	14	15	16
29	**17**	18	19	20	21	22	23
30	**24**	25	26	27	28	29	30
31	**31**						

10 | Sunday

11 Monday

12 Tuesday

Although we cannot control God's time, it is part
of the human condition to want to receive the
thing we are waiting for as quickly as possible.

MANUSCRIPT FOUND IN ACCRA

Week 28

J U L Y

						1	2
27	**3**	**4**	5	6	7	8	9
28	**10**	11	12	13	14	15	16
29	**17**	18	19	20	21	22	23
30	**24**	25	26	27	28	29	30
31	**31**						

26

13 Wednesday

14 Thursday

15 Friday

16 Saturday

When God wants to drive someone mad,
he grants them their every wish.

THE VALKYRIES

						1	2
26							
27	**3**	**4**	5	6	7	8	9
28	**10**	11	12	13	14	15	16
29	**17**	18	19	20	21	22	23
30	**24**	25	26	27	28	29	30
31	**31**						

17 | Sunday

18 Monday

19 Tuesday

Love is patience.

THE SUPREME GIFT

JULY

						1	2
26							
27	**3**	**4**	5	6	7	8	9
28	**10**	11	12	13	14	15	16
29	**17**	18	19	20	21	22	23
30	**24**	25	26	27	28	29	30
31	**31**						

20 Wednesday

21 Thursday

22 | Friday

23 | Saturday

There are moments when our lives are full of
tribulations, and we cannot avoid them.
But they are there for a reason.

THE FIFTH MOUNTAIN

J U L Y

						1	2
26						1	2
27	**3**	**4**	5	6	7	8	9
28	**10**	11	12	13	14	15	16
29	**17**	18	19	20	21	22	23
30	**24**	25	26	27	28	29	30
31	**31**						

24 | Sunday

25 Monday

26 Tuesday

Love can only survive when
you have some hope—however remote—
of winning over your beloved.

BY THE RIVER PIEDRA I SAT DOWN AND WEPT

J U LY

26						1	2
27	**3**	**4**	5	6	7	8	9
28	**10**	11	12	13	14	15	16
29	**17**	18	19	20	21	22	23
30	**24**	25	26	27	28	29	30
31	**31**						

27 | Wednesday

28 | Thursday

29 Friday

---

30 Saturday

Why is patience so important?
Because it makes us pay attention.

THE WITCH OF PORTOBELLO

Week 31

JULY

26					1	2
27	**3**	**4**	5	6	7	8	9
28	**10**	11	12	13	14	15	16
29	**17**	18	19	20	21	22	23
30	**24**	25	26	27	28	29	30
31	**31**						

31 | Sunday

AUGUST

Vital

The Extraordinary resides
in the Path of Ordinary People.
Today, this understanding is the most
precious thing I have in life; it is what
allows me to do anything and will
always accompany me.

THE PILGRIMAGE

1 | Monday

2 | Tuesday

Listen to your guardian angel. Transform yourself.
Be a warrior, and be happy as you fight the good
fight.

BY THE RIVER PIEDRA I SAT DOWN AND WEPT

31		1	2	3	4	5	6
32	**7**	8	9	10	11	12	13
33	**14**	15	16	17	18	19	20
34	**21**	22	23	24	25	26	27
35	**28**	29	30	31			

3 Wednesday

4 Thursday

5 Friday

6 Saturday

We need a very clear goal for any given step.

ADULTERY

Week 32

31		1	2	3	4	5	6
32	**7**	8	9	10	11	12	13
33	**14**	15	16	17	18	19	20
34	**21**	22	23	24	25	26	27
35	**28**	29	30	31			

7 Sunday

8 Monday

9 Tuesday

If you want to be creative, try to forget
that you have all that experience.

THE WINNER STANDS ALONE

31		1	2	3	4	5	6
32	**7**	8	9	10	11	12	13
33	**14**	15	16	17	18	19	20
34	**21**	22	23	24	25	26	27
35	**28**	29	30	31			

10 Wednesday

11 Thursday

12 | Friday

13 | Saturday

Love does not ask many questions because
if we start to think, we start to feel afraid.

BY THE RIVER PIEDRA I SAT DOWN AND WEPT

AUGUST

31		1	2	3	4	5	6
32	**7**	8	9	10	11	12	13
33	**14**	15	16	17	18	19	20
34	**21**	22	23	24	25	26	27
35	**28**	29	30	31			

14 | Sunday

15 | Monday

16 | Tuesday

Those who always try to find an explanation
for magical and mysterious human relationships
will miss the best part of life.

ADULTERY

31		1	2	3	4	5	6
32	**7**	8	9	10	11	12	13
33	**14**	15	16	17	18	19	20
34	**21**	22	23	24	25	26	27
35	**28**	29	30	31			

17 | Wednesday

18 | Thursday

19 Friday

20 Saturday

Love is the true secret of life.

THE SUPREME GIFT

31		1	2	3	4	5	6
32	**7**	8	9	10	11	12	13
33	**14**	15	16	17	18	19	20
34	**21**	22	23	24	25	26	27
35	**28**	29	30	31			

21 Sunday

22 Monday

23 Tuesday

We are born from a seed, we grow, we age,
we die, we return to the earth and again become
the seed that, sooner or later, becomes
reincarnate in another person.

HIPPIE

Week 34

31		1	2	3	4	5	6
32	**7**	8	9	10	11	12	13
33	**14**	15	16	17	18	19	20
34	**21**	22	23	24	25	26	27
35	**28**	29	30	31			

24 | Wednesday

25 | Thursday

26 Friday

27 Saturday

No one can lie, no one can hide anything,
when they look directly into someone's eyes.

BY THE RIVER PIEDRA I SAT DOWN AND WEPT

AUGUST

31		1	2	3	4	5	6
32	**7**	8	9	10	11	12	13
33	**14**	15	16	17	18	19	20
34	**21**	22	23	24	25	26	27
35	**28**	29	30	31			

28 Sunday

29 | Monday

30 | Tuesday

Anyone who stands outside the Door of Problems
and fails to recognize it may well end up leaving
it open and allowing tragedies to enter.

THE WINNER STANDS ALONE

AUGUST

31		1	2	3	4	5	6
32	**7**	8	9	10	11	12	13
33	**14**	15	16	17	18	19	20
34	**21**	22	23	24	25	26	27
35	**28**	29	30	31			

31 | Wednesday

SEPTEMBER

Tenderness

True love is an act
of total surrender.

**BY THE RIVER PIEDRA
I SAT DOWN AND WEPT**

If you love someone, then you want your beloved to be happy.
You might feel frightened for them initially, but that feeling
soon gives way to pride at seeing them doing what they want
to do, and going where they always dreamed of going.

MANUSCRIPT FOUND IN ACCRA

Week 35

35					1	2	3
36	**4**	**5**	6	7	8	9	10
37	**11**	12	13	14	15	16	17
38	**18**	19	20	21	22	23	24
39	**25**	26	27	28	29	30	

1 | Thursday

2 Friday

3 Saturday

Fear makes us ashamed of showing our love.

BY THE RIVER PIEDRA I SAT DOWN AND WEPT

35					1	2	3
36	**4**	**5**	6	7	8	9	10
37	**11**	12	13	14	15	16	17
38	**18**	19	20	21	22	23	24
39	**25**	26	27	28	29	30	

4 Sunday

5 Monday

6 Tuesday

Happiness does not breed in captivity
nor does it diminish when it is given away.
On the contrary, merely by sowing happiness,
we increase our quota.

THE SUPREME GIFT

35				1	2	3
36	**4**	**5**	6	7	8	9	10
37	**11**	12	13	14	15	16	17
38	**18**	19	20	21	22	23	24
39	**25**	26	27	28	29	30

7 Wednesday

8 Thursday

9 | Friday

10 | Saturday

For the first time, I will smile without feeling guilty,
because joy is not a sin.

MANUSCRIPT FOUND IN ACCRA

SEPTEMBER

35				1	2	3
36	**4**	**5**	6	7	8	9	10
37	**11**	12	13	14	15	16	17
38	**18**	19	20	21	22	23	24
39	**25**	26	27	28	29	30

11 Sunday

12 Monday

13 Tuesday

The Warrior of the Light views life with
tenderness and determination.

WARRIOR OF LIGHT

SEPTEMBER

35					1	2	3
36	**4**	**5**	6	7	8	9	10
37	**11**	12	13	14	15	16	17
38	**18**	19	20	21	22	23	24
39	**25**	26	27	28	29	30	

14 | Wednesday

15 | Thursday

16 | Friday

17 | Saturday

Tenderness is one of the main
characteristics of love.

MAKTUB

35					1	2	3
36	**4**	**5**	6	7	8	9	10
37	**11**	12	13	14	15	16	17
38	**18**	19	20	21	22	23	24
39	**25**	26	27	28	29	30	

18 | Sunday

19 Monday

20 Tuesday

Nothing else in the world matters—only love.
This was the love that Jesus felt for humanity.

THE PILGRIMAGE

35					1	2	3
36	**4**	**5**	6	7	8	9	10
37	**11**	12	13	14	15	16	17
38	**18**	19	20	21	22	23	24
39	**25**	26	27	28	29	30	

21 Wednesday

22 Thursday

23 Friday

24 Saturday

Help us to be humble when we receive and joyful
when we give.

MANUSCRIPT FOUND IN ACCRA

SEPTEMBER

					1	2	3
35							
36	**4**	**5**	6	7	8	9	10
37	**11**	12	13	14	15	16	17
38	**18**	19	20	21	22	23	24
39	**25**	26	27	28	29	30	

25 Sunday

26 Monday

27 Tuesday

Our time on this earth is sacred, and we should
celebrate every moment.

THE WITCH OF PORTOBELLO

SEPTEMBER

35					1	2	3
36	**4**	**5**	6	7	8	9	10
37	**11**	12	13	14	15	16	17
38	**18**	19	20	21	22	23	24
39	**25**	26	27	28	29	30	

28 | Wednesday

29 | Thursday

30 Friday

When a soul acts in accordance with its dreams,
this fills God with joy.

MAKTUB

SEPTEMBER

35					1	2	3
36	**4**	**5**	6	7	8	9	10
37	**11**	12	13	14	15	16	17
38	**18**	19	20	21	22	23	24
39	**25**	26	27	28	29	30	

OCTOBER

Indispensable

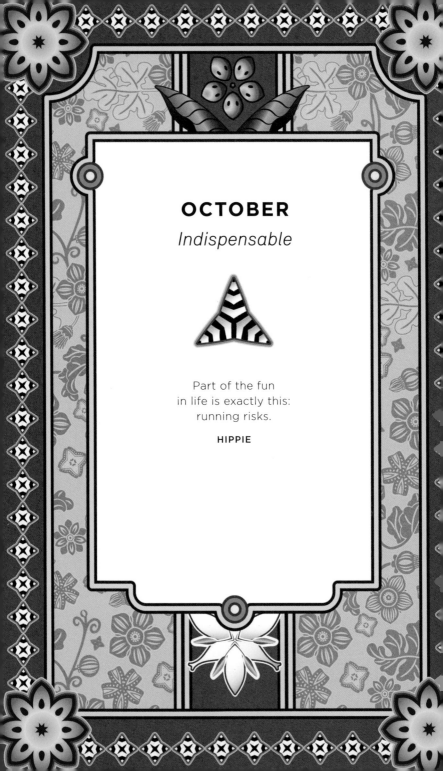

Part of the fun
in life is exactly this:
running risks.

HIPPIE

1 | Saturday

Once something is written,
it cannot be avoided.

THE ALCHEMIST

OCTOBER

39							1
40	**2**	3	4	5	6	7	8
41	**9**	**10**	11	12	13	14	15
42	**16**	17	18	19	20	21	22
43	**23**	24	25	26	27	28	29
44	**30**	31					

2 | Sunday

3 Monday

4 Tuesday

Along with the birth of love came a need to find
an answer to the mystery of existence.

ALEPH

Week 40

39							1
40	**2**	3	4	5	6	7	8
41	**9**	**10**	11	12	13	14	15
42	**16**	17	18	19	20	21	22
43	**23**	24	25	26	27	28	29
44	**30**	31					

5 Wednesday

6 Thursday

7 Friday

8 Saturday

Receiving is also an act of love. Allowing someone
else to make us happy will make them happy, too.

MANUSCRIPT FOUND IN ACCRA

39							1
40	**2**	3	4	5	6	7	8
41	**9**	**10**	11	12	13	14	15
42	**16**	17	18	19	20	21	22
43	**23**	24	25	26	27	28	29
44	**30**	31					

9 | Sunday

10 | Monday

11 | Tuesday

It's not necessary to move mountains
in order to prove one's faith.

BY THE RIVER PIEDRA I SAT DOWN AND WEPT

OCTOBER

39						1
40	**2**	3	4	5	6	7	8
41	**9**	**10**	11	12	13	14	15
42	**16**	17	18	19	20	21	22
43	**23**	24	25	26	27	28	29
44	**30**	31				

12 | Wednesday

13 | Thursday

14 Friday

15 Saturday

If you start out by promising what you don't even
have yet, you'll lose your desire to work
towards achieving it.

THE ALCHEMIST

39						1
40	**2**	3	4	5	6	7	8
41	**9**	**10**	11	12	13	14	15
42	**16**	17	18	19	20	21	22
43	**23**	24	25	26	27	28	29
44	**30**	31				

16 Sunday

17 Monday

18 Tuesday

I need to take risks. I need to lose
my fear of defeat.

BRIDA

Week 42

39							1
40	**2**	3	4	5	6	7	8
41	**9**	**10**	11	12	13	14	15
42	**16**	17	18	19	20	21	22
43	**23**	24	25	26	27	28	29
44	**30**	31					

19 | Wednesday

20 | Thursday

21 Friday

22 Saturday

A divided kingdom cannot defend
itself against its adversaries.

BY THE RIVER PIEDRA I SAT DOWN AND WEPT

39							1
40	**2**	3	4	5	6	7	8
41	**9**	**10**	11	12	13	14	15
42	**16**	17	18	19	20	21	22
43	**23**	24	25	26	27	28	29
44	**30**	31					

23 | Sunday

24 Monday

25 Tuesday

I had always been a warrior, facing my battles
without any bitterness; they were part of life.

THE SPY

39							1
40	**2**	3	4	5	6	7	8
41	**9**	**10**	11	12	13	14	15
42	**16**	17	18	19	20	21	22
43	**23**	24	25	26	27	28	29
44	**30**	31					

26 Wednesday

27 Thursday

28 Friday

29 Saturday

When we postpone the harvest, the fruit rots.

THE FIFTH MOUNTAIN

OCTOBER

39							1
40	**2**	3	4	5	6	7	8
41	**9**	**10**	11	12	13	14	15
42	**16**	17	18	19	20	21	22
43	**23**	24	25	26	27	28	29
44	**30**	31					

30 | Sunday

31 Monday

May I be capable of accepting myself as I am:
a person who walks and feels and talks like anyone else,
but who, despite his faults, is also brave.

MANUSCRIPT FOUND IN ACCRA

39							1
40	**2**	3	4	5	6	7	8
41	**9**	**10**	11	12	13	14	15
42	**16**	17	18	19	20	21	22
43	**23**	24	25	26	27	28	29
44	**30**	31					

NOVEMBER

Nobility

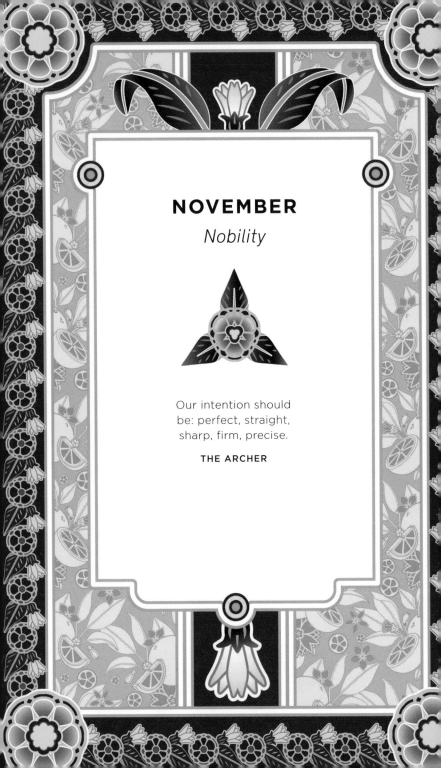

Our intention should
be: perfect, straight,
sharp, firm, precise.

THE ARCHER

1 Tuesday

The only way to make the right decision is
knowing what would be the wrong decision.

THE PILGRIMAGE

44			1	2	3	4	5
45	**6**	7	8	9	10	**11**	12
46	**13**	14	15	16	17	18	19
47	**20**	21	22	23	**24**	25	26
48	**27**	28	29	30			

2 Wednesday

3 Thursday

4 Friday

5 Saturday

Whenever you feel that your soul is not contented,
do not ask for advice, but take the necessary decisions
to keep you going on your journey through life.

MAKTUB

NOVEMBER

44		1	2	3	4	5
45	**6**	7	8	9	10	**11**	12
46	**13**	14	15	16	17	18	19
47	**20**	21	22	23	**24**	25	26
48	**27**	28	29	30		

6 | Sunday

7 | Monday

8 | Tuesday

Freedom: feeling whatever your heart wants to
feel regardless of what other people think.

THE FIFTH MOUNTAIN

44		1	2	3	4	5
45	**6**	7	8	9	10	**11**	12
46	**13**	14	15	16	17	18	19
47	**20**	21	22	23	**24**	25	26
48	**27**	28	29	30			

9 | Wednesday

10 | Thursday

11 | Friday

12 | Saturday

A gift is a grace, or a mercy, but it is also a mercy
to know how to lead one's life with dignity,
hard work, and love for one's fellows.

BY THE RIVER PIEDRA I SAT DOWN AND WEPT

NOVEMBER

44		1	2	3	4	5
45	**6**	7	8	9	10	**11**	12
46	**13**	14	15	16	17	18	19
47	**20**	21	22	23	**24**	25	26
48	**27**	28	29	30

13 Sunday

14 Monday

15 Tuesday

Going into combat is an act of love. The enemy
helps us to grow and develop, they hone us.

THE PILGRIMAGE

Week 46

NOVEMBER

44		1	2	3	4	5
45	**6**	7	8	9	10	**11**	12
46	**13**	14	15	16	17	18	19
47	**20**	21	22	23	**24**	25	26
48	**27**	28	29	30			

16 | Wednesday

17 | Thursday

18 Friday

19 Saturday

The universe always helps us fight for our dreams,
no matter how foolish they may seem.

BY THE RIVER PIEDRA I SAT DOWN AND WEPT

NOVEMBER

44		1	2	3	4	5
45	**6**	7	8	9	10	**11**	12
46	**13**	14	15	16	17	18	19
47	**20**	21	22	23	**24**	25	26
48	**27**	28	29	30		

20 | Sunday

21 Monday

22 Tuesday

Every path is unique and every destiny
is unique to the individual.

THE WITCH OF PORTOBELLO

NOVEMBER

44		1	2	3	4	5
45	**6**	7	8	9	10	**11**	12
46	**13**	14	15	16	17	18	19
47	**20**	21	22	23	**24**	25	26
48	**27**	28	29	30			

23 Wednesday

24 Thursday

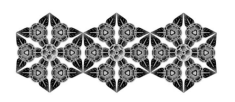

25 Friday

26 Saturday

I was able to learn from the simplest
and most unexpected things, such as the stories
parents tell their children.

HIPPIE

NOVEMBER

44		1	2	3	4	5
45	**6**	7	8	9	10	**11**	12
46	**13**	14	15	16	17	18	19
47	**20**	21	22	23	**24**	25	26
48	**27**	28	29	30		

27 | Sunday

28 Monday

29 Tuesday

Not knowing what decision to take
is the most painful of afflictions.

BY THE RIVER PIEDRA I SAT DOWN AND WEPT

NOVEMBER

44		1	2	3	4	5
45	**6**	7	8	9	10	**11**	12
46	**13**	14	15	16	17	18	19
47	**20**	21	22	23	**24**	25	26
48	**27**	28	29	30		

30 | Wednesday

DECEMBER

Beauty

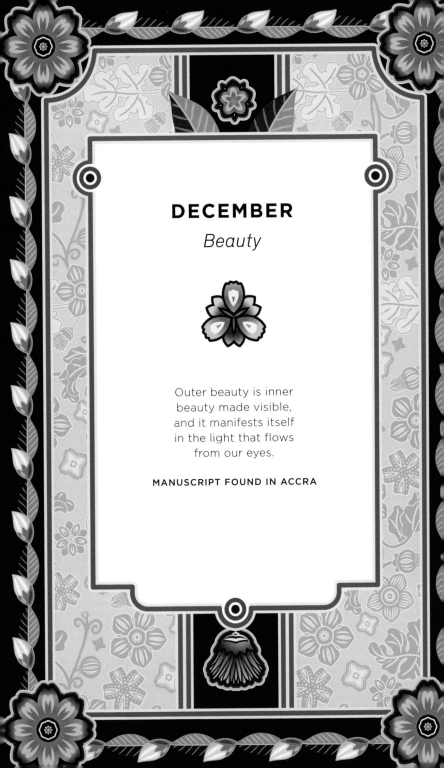

Outer beauty is inner
beauty made visible,
and it manifests itself
in the light that flows
from our eyes.

MANUSCRIPT FOUND IN ACCRA

Elegance is not something superficial,
but the way in which a man can do honor
to his life and his work.

THE ARCHER

48					1	2	3
49	**4**	5	6	7	8	9	10
50	**11**	12	13	14	15	16	17
51	**18**	19	20	21	22	23	24
52	**25**	26	27	28	29	30	31

1 | Thursday

2 | Friday

3 | Saturday

The simpler and more sober the posture,
the more beautiful.

THE WITCH OF PORTOBELLO

Week 49

48					1	2	3
49	**4**	5	6	7	8	9	10
50	**11**	12	13	14	15	16	17
51	**18**	19	20	21	22	23	24
52	**25**	26	27	28	29	30	31

4 | Sunday

5 | Monday

6 | Tuesday

The world is a mirror and reflects back
to us our own face.

WARRIOR OF LIGHT

DECEMBER

						1	2	3
48						1	2	3
49	**4**	5	6	7	8	9	10
50	**11**	12	13	14	15	16	17
51	**18**	19	20	21	22	23	24
52	**25**	26	27	28	29	30	31

7 | Wednesday

8 | Thursday

9 Friday

10 Saturday

At times, when loneliness seems to crush all
beauty, the only way to resist is to remain open.

LIKE THE FLOWING RIVER

Week 50

DECEMBER

48				1	2	3
49	**4**	5	6	7	8	9	10
50	**11**	12	13	14	15	16	17
51	**18**	19	20	21	22	23	24
52	**25**	26	27	28	29	30	31

11 Sunday

12 Monday

13 Tuesday

Elegance is the correct posture if the writing
is to be perfect. It's the same with life.

THE WITCH OF PORTOBELLO

Week 50

48				1	2	3
49	**4**	5	6	7	8	9	10
50	**11**	12	13	14	15	16	17
51	**18**	19	20	21	22	23	24
52	**25**	26	27	28	29	30	31

14 Wednesday

15 Thursday

16 Friday

17 Saturday

In order to be capable of seeing what is beautiful,
we must carry beauty within ourselves.

WARRIOR OF LIGHT

DECEMBER

48					1	2	3
49	**4**	5	6	7	8	9	10
50	**11**	12	13	14	15	16	17
51	**18**	19	20	21	22	23	24
52	**25**	26	27	28	29	30	31

18 | Sunday

19 Monday

20 Tuesday

You cannot judge the beauty of a particular
path just by looking at the gate.

LIKE THE FLOWING RIVER

DECEMBER

48					1	2	3
49	**4**	5	6	7	8	9	10
50	**11**	12	13	14	15	16	17
51	**18**	19	20	21	22	23	24
52	**25**	26	27	28	29	30	31

21 | Wednesday

22 | Thursday

23 Friday

24 Saturday

Happiness is something that multiplies
when shared.

BY THE RIVER PIEDRA I SAT DOWN AND WEPT

DECEMBER

48				1	2	3
49	**4**	5	6	7	8	9	10
50	**11**	12	13	14	15	16	17
51	**18**	19	20	21	22	23	24
52	**25**	26	27	28	29	30	31

25 Sunday

26 Monday

27 Tuesday

There's nothing wrong with doing simple things.

THE WITCH OF PORTOBELLO

DECEMBER

48					1	2	3
49	**4**	5	6	7	8	9	10
50	**11**	12	13	14	15	16	17
51	**18**	19	20	21	22	23	24
52	**25**	26	27	28	29	30	31

28 | Wednesday

29 | Thursday

30 Friday

31 Saturday

Beauty exists not in sameness but in difference.

MANUSCRIPT FOUND IN ACCRA

DECEMBER

48					1	2	3
49	**4**	5	6	7	8	9	10
50	**11**	12	13	14	15	16	17
51	**18**	19	20	21	22	23	24
52	**25**	26	27	28	29	30	31

Original title: *Simplicidade 2022*

Copyright © 2021 by Paulo Coelho and Mosaikk AS
http://paulocoelhoblog.com/

All rights reserved. Published in the United States of America by Vintage Books, a division of Penguin Random House LLC, New York, and distributed in Canada by Random House of Canada, a division of Penguin Random House Canada Limited, Toronto.

Published by arrangement with Sant Jordi Asociados, Agencia Literaria, S.L.U., Barcelona (Spain). www.santjordi-asociados.com

Vintage is a registered trademark and Vintage International and the colophon are trademarks of Penguin Random House LLC.

Vintage ISBN: 978-0-593-31517-0

Quote selection: Márcia Botelho
Translation copyright © Margaret Jull Costa
Illustrations by Catalina Estrada, www.catalinaestrada.com
Author photograph © Paul Macleod
Design by Lene Stangebye Geving / Mireia Barreras

www.vintagebooks.com

Printed and bound by TBB, a. s., Slovakia, 2021

First Vintage International edition: July 2021